THE
GARDEN

D0192821

WES PORTER
Illustrated by Joe Weissmann

A Somerville House Book

WORKMAN PUBLISHING
NEW YORK

*To my son Marcus, a young gardener,
for giving me time to write this book.*

*Special thanks to Freek Vrugtman, The
Royal Botanical Gardens, Mother Goose
Media and Eva Hoepfner.*

Library of Congress
Cataloging-in-Publication Data
Porter, Wes.
    The garden book & the
    greenhouse.
    "A Somerville House book."
    Summary: Provides tips on how to
plant and cultivate a variety of
vegetables, flowers, and indoor plants.
    1. Gardening—Juvenile
literature.   [1. Gardening]
I. Weissmann, Joe, ill.   II. Title
III. Title: Garden book and the
greenhouse.
SB457.P67   1989   635   89-40372
ISBN 0-89480-346-8

Workman Publishing
708 Broadway
New York, New York 10003

Printed in the United States of America

First printing October 1989

10 9 8 7 6 5 4 3 2 1

Contents

B efore you can grow plants in the Greenhouse, you'll probably have to visit a nursery or one of the garden centers located at hardware or department stores or supermarkets. Or write to seed manufacturers and ask them to mail you their catalogs so you can order direct from them. Check the requirements of the plants you want to grow before making your purchases.

SUPPLIES

Seed packets
Soil-less mix (or vermiculite, peatmoss and limestone to make your own)
Peat pellets (Jiffy 7s)
Liquid and/or dry fertilizer
Bird sand
Compost

TOOLS AND UTENSILS

Pots and other containers
Measuring cup
Mister or watering can
Trowel
Hoe
Square-nosed spade
Gravel rake

Grow Some Surprises

Plants are everywhere! Just look around you, and you're likely to see a plant growing nearby—a potted African violet on the windowsill, perhaps, or a blade of grass on the lawn, or even a giant sunflower nodding down at you from the vegetable garden.

Found in every part of the world, plants come in all shapes and sizes. Many have been cultivated throughout the centuries, providing us with sustenance and delighting us with their beauty.

Become a gardener yourself and discover how surprising plants can be. Sow some polkadot seeds in your Greenhouse to grow a plant with freckles that fade in the shade and brighten in the sun. Transplant some cactus to grow a prickly desert garden right in your own room. Or start some peanut bushes and watch their tiny yellow flowers actually poke underground.

Browse through The Garden Book and choose the plants that excite you. Then dig in—fill the starter tray, sow some seeds and harvest some fun. Happy gardening!

What Is a Plant?

Imagine! Without the oxygen and food supplied by plants, we wouldn't even be here! From tiny, floating algae to towering redwood trees, plants are an essential part of life on our planet. They can't move from place to place the way we do, of course, and they lack sense organs like our eyes and ears, yet plants are extremely responsive to the conditions around them.

While many species grow from seeds, the mosses and ferns begin as dust-like spores. And while most plants are green, mushrooms are brown or white because they lack the green pigment called chlorophyll. But all

plants, like human beings, have the ability to reproduce, or create new organisms just like themselves.

In order to appreciate plants, and to care for them properly, it's important to understand how they live and how each part contributes to their survival.

Every plant, whether it's a fragile petunia seedling or a big, bushy tomato plant, needs light, water and soil in order to flourish. But different plants require different amounts of these three essentials, and it will be up to you—the gardener—to give your plants just what they need to grow strong and well.

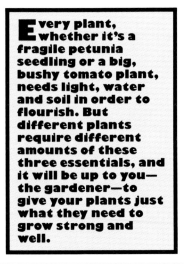

At the center of the flower lies the plant's reproductive parts, usually consisting of a pistil (female) and stamens (male).

The plant's stem supports its leaves and flowers. Through tiny tubes in the main growing stem, water and dissolved minerals from the roots travel to smaller stems that lead to the leaves themselves. The food made in the leaves then moves back downward to nourish all other parts of the plant.

Cross section of a plant stem.

The leaf is a food factory! Here, the raw ingredients carried up through the stems combine with the air to make the sugary substance that feeds the plant. This amazing process, known as photosynthesis, is made possible by the energy from sunlight and the leaf's chlorophyll.

Roots not only anchor the plant, but also take in water and dissolved minerals from the soil.

7

Greenhouse Basics

Use your Greenhouse to grow plants from seeds, cuttings or bulbs—or turn it into a terrarium with its own miniature landscape! The clear Greenhouse roof lets in light, allows ventilation through small air vents, and prevents heat and moisture from escaping. The sturdy plastic "starter tray" is designed without drainage holes to keep mess to a minimum. (Normally, good drainage is important for plant roots, but your seedlings can do without it for the short time they spend in the tray *as long as you don't overwater them.*)

By controlling the environment of your tiny new plants, you'll give them the best chance to flourish at a time when they are most vulnerable to weather, disease and insect attack.

Soil

The most important thing you can do for your plants is to give them good soil, rich in nutrients. Finding the right soil for your Greenhouse is an easy matter: all you need is some soil-less mix, which doesn't contain any soil at all! This mix is disease-free and is therefore very safe for delicate new seedlings or cuttings.

You can also use peat pellets, such as Jiffy 7s, for larger seeds and cuttings. Combining both soil and peat, these compact pellets expand when soaked in water.

MAKE YOUR OWN SOIL-LESS MIX

Combine the following in a plastic garbage bag:

4 quarts of vermiculite
4 quarts of peat moss
2 level tablespoons of ground limestone

At planting time, fill starter tray and add warm water until mix is moist throughout.

Seeds

All the different kinds of seeds to choose from might be overwhelming at first. There can be many varieties of each plant species. "Cultivars" are *var*ieties that have been *culti*vated by gardeners in the past to strengthen the original plant or to alter its shape or coloring. Six cultivars of the marigold, for instance, are listed on page 47 as appropriate choices for your Greenhouse.

Read through the plant pages to find the species and cultivars that are best suited to your locale (see the Plant Symbols chart on page 11), then look for their names among the seed packets at the garden center. The species name appears above the cultivar name on the front of each packet; on the back is information on planting.

If you're not sure which seeds to buy first, try alyssum, marigold or radish. All three germinate quickly and are good for beginning gardeners.

Cuttings

Taking cuttings from adult plants and rooting them in soil can save time and sometimes is preferable to starting out with seeds. Check the symbols at the top of each plant page to see whether or not cuttings are recommended.

Place the Greenhouse in a window facing north or east, so your young plants won't get a sunburn.

If you decide on this growing method, ask a neighbor if you can take a stem cutting from one of his or her adult plants. Cut a 2″ to 3″ tip (the end of the stem that's still growing) from the plant and trim it just below the lowest leaf; cut off the flowers, buds and all the leaves except the topmost one, leaving the growing tip in place.

Bulbs

To grow crocuses or other bulbs in the starter tray or in windowsill pots, ask for bulbs that have been specially treated to bloom indoors. For more on bulbs, see page 48.

Leave the growing tip and topmost leaf when you take a cutting.

FERTILIZERS

Most fertilizers are mixtures of nitrogen (N), phosphorus (P) and potassium (K). Nitrogen helps plants to develop lots of healthy leaves, phosphorus promotes the growth of new seedlings and the production of flowers, and potassium increases hardiness and disease resistance.

Each plant in this book is marked by a symbol that tells you which element it needs most. For example, the symbol P on the snapdragon page indicates that you'll want to buy a liquid fertilizer with a high phosphorus level. Look among the fertilizers at the store, and you'll see that each one gives three numbers: the first always refers to the level of nitrogen, the second to phosphorus, and the third to potassium. A package marked "0–15–14" would indicate that the phosphorus level (the second number) is highest in that particular fertilizer.

There are both chemical and natural fertilizers to choose from. While plants don't know the difference between the two types, natural fertilizers are made from natural substances and are therefore preferred.

Plant Symbols

L ook for the following symbols next to the name of each plant in the book. These symbols will tell you the best method of starting each plant, how much sun and water it needs, and which type of fertilizer to use.

How to start your plants.	What your plants need.
Seeds	Bright sunlight
Bulbs	Partial sunlight
Stem cuttings	Shade
Leaf cuttings	Light watering
	Medium watering
	Heavy watering
	Dry powdered fertilizer
	Liquid fertilizer high in nitrogen
	Liquid fertilizer high in phosphates

Planting Time!

Now that you know the basics, you're ready to garden. To give your plants the best growing environment, be sure to follow the planting instructions given in the book and any further directions printed on the seed packets.

1. Fill the starter tray of your Greenhouse almost to the top with soil-less mix, or soak up to 6 peat pellets in the tray.

For seeds: Sow according to the instructions given for each plant. Often there will be more seeds in the packet than you need; keep unused seeds in a sealed jar in a cool, dark place.

For cuttings: Poke a hole about ½″ deep in the soil-less mix or in an expanded peat pellet, and set the cut end into the hole. Firm the soil around the stem.

How to Use Peat Pellets

Soak up to 6 pellets about 10 minutes before planting seeds or cuttings. Once the pellets have popped up and expanded, poke a hole ½″ deep in each one and plant 2 seeds or a single cutting according to the directions given on the plant pages. (Sowing 2 seeds will double your chance of success.)

2. Lightly water your newly planted seeds or cuttings, letting the moisture seep into the soil-less mix or peat pellets, then sprinkle again until the mix or pellets are soaked through. Lift the starter tray to feel how heavy it is; knowing the tray's normal weight will help you later in determining whether or not your plants need water.

3. Put the roof on and place the Greenhouse in a warm location. A windowsill is best, facing either north (away from the sun) or east (toward the morning sun).

Always use soil-less mix in your Greenhouse tray—never garden soil.

Poke the end of your cutting into a moistened peat pellet.

4. Every day, lift your Greenhouse to see if more water is needed. If it feels light, your plants are thirsty. Be kind when watering! Plants don't like cold showers any more than you do, so always use water at room temperature. Beware: overwatering results in airless soil, rotting roots, and wilting.

5. Watch for the seeds to sprout within the germination time given on the plant page or seed packet. (If there are no signs of life a week past the germination time, start again!) When the seeds have become seedlings, move the Greenhouse to a north or east window. Never put young seedlings or cuttings in a place that receives direct sunlight, because too much heat and light will "cook" them.

6. The starter tray, as its name implies, is used only to get your plants started. Before long, they'll have to be moved to larger quarters.

For seedlings: When the second pair of leaves (actually the first *real* pair of leaves after the "seed leaves") appears on the seedlings, it's time to transplant.

For cuttings: To tell if a cutting has rooted, tug gently on the leaves. If you feel resistance, the cutting is ready for transplanting; if not, let it grow a while longer in the tray. Rooting can take from 3 to 8 weeks.

MISTERS ARE BEST

To disturb your seeds as little as possible and to avoid overwatering, use a mister instead of a watering can. Simply fill a laundry sprinkler, small spritzer or spray bottle with water at room temperature. Then spray the soil-less mix or peat pellets until thoroughly soaked.

Using a mister is a safe way to water seeds and seedlings.

Germination

G ermination is the wondrous process in which a seed starts to grow. Each seed contains the embryo, or "blueprint," of the parent plant, plus nourishment that keeps the embryo alive until it can grow roots and leaves to make its own food. Protected by the hard seed coat, the tiny embryo will remain intact as long as the seed itself is kept dry, cool, free of insects and in the dark.

From seed to seedling!

Add water and warmth, and *presto!*—the outer covering softens and the embryo swells. Soon a tiny root pushes its way through the outer covering and begins to take in water and nutrients to nourish the growth of the first tiny shoot. As the shoot pushes its way upward, the root tip, covered by almost invisible hairs, pushes downward. Soon the shoot breaks through the soil surface. Now little "seed leaves" sprout, which give the plant a chance to make food for the very first time. The seed has now turned into a seedling and is well on its way to becoming an adult plant.

From Beans to Sprouts

Watch germination in action by sprouting some mung bean seeds in water. Most seeds do not need soil in order to germinate—just water and, in some cases, darkness. (Of course, soil is essential if plants are to grow to adulthood.)

Spread ¼ cup of mung beans in the starter tray and add just enough water to cover them. Put the roof on and set the Greenhouse in a warm, dark place. The next morning, drain the beans in a sieve and observe how swollen they are. This means that germination has begun.

Look inside a seed. Split open one of the beans that you've soaked overnight. The outer seed coat should peel off easily with your fingernail. Inside, you'll find a tiny root and shoot curved around a large supply of food, which forms the bulk of the seed.

Bean sprouts are perfect for snack time.

Grow beans for a snack! Rinse the beans thoroughly under cold water, return them to the starter tray, cover with the Greenhouse roof and set back in the warm, dark place. Repeat these steps 2 or 3 times a day for about 5 days. Watch for the tiny roots to push through the seed coats, followed by the shoots. At this stage, you can pick out the "husks," or pieces of seed coat, and munch a bunch of sprouts!

Transplanting to Containers

Make sure each seedling or young plant is healthy and strong before moving it from the starter tray. Discard any undersize or unhealthy-looking plants, and throw away the used soil-less mix. Clay or plastic pots, 3″ in diameter, are best at this stage of the growing process. (If the pots are too big, the roots can't absorb all the moisture because too much soil surrounds them.) Clean paper cups or plastic milk and juice containers also work well for transplanting; ask an adult to help you cut off the tops and punch holes in the sides just above the base.

Transplanting to containers can be quick and easy if you follow the steps below.

1. Partially fill each container with fresh soil-less mix. Use your finger to poke a hole, knuckle-deep, in the mix of each one.

2. To remove a plant from the starter tray, push a pencil into the soil to one side of the stem. Coax the plant upward while tugging gently on the leaves—*not on the stem*—until it's free from the soil. Now place it in the hole with its roots and root tips straight down, not twisted or turned up, and gently fill in around the roots with more mix. Press the soil firmly down around the roots.

3. Slowly add water until you see it run out through the holes.

4. Repeat for each plant.

> ## Peat Pots
>
> If you've started your plants in peat pellets, you don't have to transplant them into small pots. The expanded pellets become "little pots" themselves and can be transplanted directly into big containers filled with soil-less mix or into the soil of your outdoor garden.

Handle seedlings by the leaves, not by the stems.

5. Ask an adult to mix a table-spoon of bleach into a half-gallon of water. Scrub the starter tray well, then soak it in the bleach solution for half an hour. Rinse well and leave to dry overnight before using again.

6. Give plants the light, moisture and fertilizer indicated by the symbols on the plant pages.

7. As your plants outgrow their containers, move them to larger quarters in pots, tubs or window-boxes filled with soil-less mix. For outdoor locations, follow the "hardening off" directions on page 18.

8. Outdoor containers may have to be watered once a day, or sometimes twice a day, as the wind and sun dry out the soil in

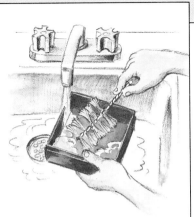

Be sure to clean the tray between each planting.

When plants outgrow their containers, it's time to transplant them into bigger pots or the outdoor garden.

THINNING

Gardeners "thin" to prevent overcrowding in containers or garden plots, which can lead to stunted, sickly plants. Use a pair of sewing scissors to clip the unwanted plants close to the ground. (This way, you won't disturb the roots of the remaining plants.)

windowboxes, baskets and barrels much more quickly. For containers, give the soil enough water to keep it continually moist but not as wet as a swamp. You may want to invest in a moisture meter, which will tell you when the soil is still damp at the bottom of the pot—even if it's bone-dry on top. Water only when the meter says to.

Transplanting to the Outdoor Garden

Y ou might have to work a little harder to plant an outdoor garden but it's well worth the effort! Wear your oldest clothes, a beat-up pair of shoes and maybe some gloves to make washing up easier.

Hardening Off

Whether in the Greenhouse or in small pots inside, your plants have lived in a carefully controlled environment and now must get used to the outdoors. A week before transplanting, let the plants sit outside in a sheltered, shady place in the daytime and bring them in at night. This will greatly help them adjust to their new surroundings.

Dig in compost to prepare the soil.

Preparing the Soil

Before transplanting seedlings or young plants to a good-size garden patch (see pages 62–64), you must first "doctor" the soil with compost for proper texture and fertilizer for extra nutrition. Compost is man-made *humus,* a substance that forms naturally in the soil from decayed organic materials and helps to keep it light and "crumbly." Bagged compost is available at garden centers. (Or see facing page.) Spread it 2″ to 3″ thick over the soil of your garden.

> **B**eware! Your plants can be killed by frost when the temperature dips below 32° F. Find out the last probable date for a spring frost in your area, and transplant to the outdoors after this date. Bring plants inside several weeks ahead of the first fall frost.

Ask an adult to dig the compost into the soil with a square-nosed spade while you add in dry fertilizer. One cupful per square yard is a good estimate, unless you're growing nasturtiums (see page 52) or legumes (page 35).

Remove any rocks, roots, sticks or other debris from the surface, then level the soil with a gravel rake.

Digging In

Transplant outdoors on an overcast day or in late afternoon. Moisten the seedlings or young plants before setting them out, still in their pots, in their planned location. For each plant, use a trowel to dig a hole a little bigger than its container. Holding the plant gently by the leaves with one hand, carefully slide the pot away from the roots; try not to disturb them while placing the plant and its ball of soil into the hole. Fill in around the roots with garden soil. Water with a high-phosphate liquid fertilizer to help the plant overcome "transplant shock."

Watering

Most outdoor plants require an inch of water every 3 days. If it hasn't rained heavily in that time, use a sprinkler or soaker hose in the early morning. (Never water in the evening, since plants that go soaking-wet into the cooler night hours are vulnerable to disease.)

HOMEMADE COMPOST

Many gardeners build their own "compost heap" from organic ingredients such as kitchen garbage, lawn clippings, fall leaves and garden waste. (Bones, meat and fat scraps do not belong in a compost heap, nor do dog and cat waste, branches or pieces of wood, paper, or anything inorganic such as metal and plastic.) These ingredients, piled up in layers in an out-of-the-way spot, are allowed to rot for several months until finally they turn into a wonderful soil booster.

Transplant in late afternoon or early evening.

LIQUID FERTILIZER

Grow Some Vegeta

Most people don't realize that vegetables are actually different *parts* of plants. Lettuce and spinach are leaves, for example, and celery stalks are stems. Corn and peas are seeds; carrots, radishes and beets are roots. Pumpkins, tomatoes and cucumbers are the parts of the plant that hold the seeds. And cauliflower and broccoli are actually flowers!

Many vegetables are easy to start in your Greenhouse. Browse through seed catalogs or seed packets at a garden center to discover all the possibilities.

Whichever vegetables you choose to grow, you'll find great satisfaction in tending the seedlings and harvesting your own delicious, garden-fresh, vitamin-rich food to highlight your menu. *Mmm-mmmm!*

DESCRIPTION: The tomato plant, once grown in Europe for decoration, first bears star-shaped yellow or purple flowers. In time, these flowers give way to the small green "fruit" that gradually grow into delicious, bright red tomatoes.

To save space in your garden, look for "staking" cultivars such as 'Ultra Sweet VFT,' 'Floramerica' and 'Better Boy VFN.' For "cherry" tomatoes, try 'Tiny Tim.' For pink tomatoes, grow 'Pink Girl'; for yellow, try 'Lemon Boy.' 'Patio Prize' is good for growing in containers on patios or terraces.

HOW TO PLANT: About 12 weeks before the last expected frost, sow seeds in peat pellets, or in soil-less mix 1″ apart and ¼″ deep. Water well. Germination time: 5–10 days.

GROWING TIPS: Four plants will keep you and your family well stocked with tomatoes. Transplant well after the last frost into 8″ pots or spaced 2′ apart in the outdoor garden. Stake each plant as explained on the facing page. As the plant grows, pinch off any shoots, or "suckers," that appear where each leaf joins the main stem. After tiny green tomatoes appear, fertilize plants every 2 weeks and water well. The tomatoes should start to ripen in 8–10 weeks, depending on the cultivar.

It's also necessary to stake tomato plants if you grow them in containers.

The Green Thumb

How to Stake Plants

Staking tomato plants, as well as cucumber, bean and pea plants, not only saves space but also keeps them off the ground and protected from slug attack.

Each stake should be 2″ square and 6′ tall. (An old hockey stick, angle iron or bamboo pole will not work.) Ask an adult to help you hammer in the stakes on the windward side of your plants, that is, where the wind usually comes from. For proper anchoring, one-third of each stake must be below the soil surface.

As the plant grows, tie it loosely to the stake with soft twine or strips of old pantyhose, using figure-8 knots. Don't forget to save your stakes from year to year.

Never wrap picked tomatoes (or other vegetables) in plastic— they can't "breathe" that way.

Use figure-8 knots to tie stems loosely to stakes.

Cucumbers.

DESCRIPTION: Originally from India, the cucumber plant is a sprawling vine covered with stubby little prickles for protection. It yields large leaves and two sets of tiny yellow flowers: first the "males" and then, starting about a week later, the "females." The second batch of flowers turn into the dark green cucumbers that are eaten raw in salads or soaked in brine to make crunchy pickles.

If you're interested in growing a cultivar bred for perfect pickles, look for 'National Pickling.' Otherwise, 'Marketmore 76,' 'Straight 8' or 'Sweetslice' will yield a bountiful harvest. 'Pot Luck' cucumbers are good for container growing.

HOW TO PLANT: About 6 weeks before the last expected frost, sow seeds in peat pellets, or in soil-less mix 1″ apart and ¼″ deep. Germination time: 5–7 days.

GROWING TIPS: Cucumber seedlings can be planted in 10″ pots or in the garden. Before transplanting to the garden, dig extra compost into the soil. The heavy vines of cucumber plants require sturdy stakes. (If you don't stake the plants, give them lots of room to spread out.) Cucumbers are mainly water, which means they need a lot of watering during their 8-week growing period. Be sure to pick your cucumbers before they're fully ripe. If you wait for them to turn yellow, they won't be as tasty and your plants won't produce any more cucumbers.

A CUCUMBER MYSTERY

Pick out a tiny new cucumber that has already lost its flower. Leave it on the vine as you slip it into a clear plastic bottle. Tie the bottle to the stake, and keep it tipped down so water won't get in. When the cucumber fills the bottle, cut it away from the vine—and nobody will know how it got there!

Lettuce

Head lettuce.

Leaf lettuce.

Sowing seeds every few weeks will give you a constant supply of fresh lettuce. This practice of "continuous sowing" can also be applied to radishes, beets, beans and peas.

DESCRIPTION: Popular since ancient times, lettuce is one of the most widely grown of the "leafy" vegetables. Most lettuce leaves are green, but 'Red Sails' and a few other cultivars are reddish. "Head" lettuce usually curls over into round balls of crisp, smooth leaves; "leaf" lettuce is looser and more upright. The leaves of both kinds can be smooth, crinkly or ruffled.

For a tightly curled head lettuce, try 'Green Lake.' 'Summer Boston' has a looser head. 'Parris Island Cos' is a long-leaf cultivar, while 'Super Prize' is a loose-leaf type.

HOW TO PLANT: Sow lettuce seeds in the starter tray about 8 weeks before the last frost. Sprinkle the seeds lightly and as evenly as possible over the entire surface of soil-less mix. Then cover with a thin layer of mix, no more than ¼″ thick, and water well. Germination time: 5–10 days.

GROWING TIPS: Thin your crop before transplanting (see page 17). Hot weather makes lettuce "bolt," or send up a tall stalk with bitter leaves, so don't transplant in the midsummer months. In the outdoor garden, plant leaf lettuce seedlings 6″ apart or head lettuce seedlings 10″ apart. For container growing, use 6″ pots, one plant per pot. Lettuce takes about 8 weeks of growing before you can start harvesting.

Zucchini, a summer squash.

DESCRIPTION: The prickly, creeping vines of the squash plant sprawl out in all directions, and half the fun is just *finding* your squash among the huge leaves.

Like cucumbers, squash plants have male and female flowers. The males, which are the first to blossom, make a wonderful snack; try them fresh from the vine or fill them with cream cheese. The female flowers give way to tiny squash, which get bigger and bigger throughout the growing season.

For summer harvesting, look for a "summer" squash, such as the skinny, dark green 'Black Jack' zucchini. Or try "winter" squash, such as big orange pumpkins ('Jack O'Lantern') or the pale, pear-shaped 'Early Butternut'; these squash can be left on the vine until the first frost, then cut off and stored in a cool, dry place. For fun, try vegetable spaghetti squash, which looks like spaghetti strands when you scoop out the cooked pulp.

HOW TO PLANT: Start 6 weeks before the last frost. Use peat pellets, or space 6 seeds evenly apart, about ½″ deep, in soilless mix. Germination time: 5–10 days.

GROWING TIPS: Allow at least a square yard in your garden for each seedling, and dig extra compost into the soil before transplanting. Three plants should give you plenty of squash. During the growing season of 2–3 months, get rid of any slugs and beetles hiding under the vines.

The Green Thumb

Grow a Monster Pumpkin

The biggest pumpkin in the world weighed over 600 pounds—enough for 300 pumpkin pies! See how close you can come to this record by growing the cultivar called 'Hungarian Mammoth.'

Start the seed indoors according to the instructions on page 26. When it's time to transplant, dig a square hole at least 2' deep in your garden. (You may need some help at this stage.) Fill the hole with compost, then mix in 4 handfuls of dry fertilizer. Heap the mix in the center of the hole, and leave it for a week; if the pile sinks, add more compost. Next, plant your seedling in the top of the compost pile and water carefully. Soon after the vine blossoms, little pumpkins will begin to form. Find the healthiest-looking one, and pinch off the other small pumpkins and flowers.

Throughout the growing season of about 4 months, wa-

Pumpkin, a winter squash.

Put an old patio slab or several bricks under your pumpkin to keep it from rotting. By October, you'll probably have your own giant jack-o'-lantern ready for Halloween!

ter the pumpkin daily, pinch off any new flowers or pumpkins, and fertilize every week.

The Root of the Matter

Without healthy roots, plants would fall over and die from lack of nourishment. There are two main types of roots: fibrous roots and taproots.

Fibrous Roots

Most of the plants in this book have small, slender fibrous roots that grow directly out of the bottom of the stem. These roots branch out through the soil like the strands of a net.

Radish seeds germinate quickly but should be sown outdoors in pots at least 6" wide or in the outdoor garden.

Green bean seeds are best sown directly in the outdoor garden. Expect germination within 5-10 days.

Taproots

Dandelion, radish and carrot plants all have taproots—long main roots with tiny, hairy roots growing from them. Dig up a dandelion, and you'll see a thin version of the taproot. Radishes and carrots, on the other hand, are swollen taproots that store the plant's food for nourishment during the winter months.

The Green Thumb

Roots in Action

Roots are strong! Spread several layers of paper towel in the starter tray. Sprinkle radish seeds on top and add enough water to soak the towel. Put the roof on and set the Greenhouse in a warm place. In a few days, the roots will have pushed through the seed coats. Look at the fuzzy hairs covering the main root. As the stem starts to grow, these hairs will be apparent only on the root tip. Watch for the roots to grow right into the paper towel.

Stubborn roots. Tape some bean seeds to the inside of the Greenhouse roof, and you'll see for yourself that roots always grow down. Ask someone to hold each seed in place while you cover it with a folded pad of paper towel and secure it with masking tape. Moisten the towel thoroughly with a mister. Then set the Greenhouse in a warm, dark place. (The darkness is important in

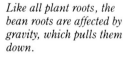

Like all plant roots, the bean roots are affected by gravity, which pulls them down.

imitating underground conditions.) Keep the towel moist and watch for root germination within 5 days. Once the roots are well established, you'll see that they point downward.

Now turn the Greenhouse roof upside down so that the roots are facing up. Count how many days it takes for the roots to change direction and turn down again.

DESCRIPTION: Easy and quick to grow in the starter tray, cress sprouts into a thick carpet of dainty, dark green leaves. Because the small, curled leaves have a hot taste, cress is sometimes known as peppergrass. It makes a snappy addition to sandwiches and salads.

HOW TO PLANT: Sprinkle the seeds lightly and as evenly as possible over the entire surface of soil-less mix in the starter tray. Press down lightly with your fingers, then water. Be careful not to wash the seeds away. Germination time: about 7 days.

Garden cress.

GROW YOUR INITIALS!

Scratch your initials in soil-less mix with the end of a spoon or mark them on the mix with baking flour. Then sprinkle cress seeds into the letter shapes and follow the planting instructions. In about 10 days, crop your initials by snipping the cress leaves at soil level with a pair of scissors.

Cress makes a fast, easy snack.

Sunflower.

Sunflowers **S**are "composed" of many tiny flowers. Each giant yellow "ray" petal and each dark floret in the center is a flower in its own right and can make a seed.

DESCRIPTION: Sunflowers are grown not just for their magnificent blooms, which actually turn to follow the path of the sun each day, but also for their delicious seeds.

Instead of regular garden sunflowers, you can plant the 'Giant Russian' cultivar and watch as the tiny seedlings grow into thick green stalks bearing huge flower heads that are often a foot wide. By the end of the growing season, your sunflowers may be well over double your height!

HOW TO PLANT: Sow seeds in peat pellets, or in soil-less mix about 1″ apart and ½″ deep. Germination time: 5–12 days.

GROWING TIPS: Transplant sunflower seedlings to a 36″ tub or barrel, or to a location in the garden where they won't shade other plants. Mix extra compost into the soil of the garden and space plants 2′ to 3′ apart. Fertilize once every 2 weeks throughout the growing season of 10–12 weeks; keep well watered.

When the florets have finished blooming and begun the transformation into the familiar black-and-white seeds, cover each seed head with an old pantyhose leg. (Squirrels and birds are keen on sunflower snacks!) After the first frost, ask an adult to help you cut off the seed heads. Then pull out the seeds and keep them in a cool, dry place, in paper bags, as a snack for yourself or for winter birds. In the latter case, begin feeding in December (there should be plenty of wild seeds until that time) and be sure to carry on until spring comes.

Herbs for All Seasons

Parsley.

Technically speaking, an herb is any plant with a soft green stem. Therefore, except for the dracaena, all the plants in this book are herbs!

In terms of gardening, however, an herb is a plant especially prized for its scent or taste. Sage or tarragon, for example, makes a cooking chicken smell irresistible. Freshly cut chives will do the same for a baked potato. For variety, sprinkle thyme on carrots or add parsley to macaroni and cheese. The fun comes in being adven-

*To speed up **parsley**'s 3-week germination period, soak seeds overnight before sowing in peat pellets or directly in the outdoor garden. The lacy, dark green leaves of this popular herb will sprout up, and soon you'll have some transplants ready for potting.*

turous and trying out new combinations of herbs and foods.

Many herbs can be grown from seeds, which usually have a long germination period of 2–3 weeks. Some, such as thyme and oregano, can be grown from cuttings. Once young plants are well established, they can be transplanted outside into containers or the outdoor garden. Outdoor gardeners should beware—many herbs are hardy and like to spread. Transplanting into 6″ pots, or bigger, curbs the herbs' tendency to spread

Chive.

***Chives** are related to onions and garlic but have a milder taste. Sow seeds in starter tray or in the outdoor garden, and expect germination within 2–3 weeks. Snip the tall, hollow leaves with scissors.*

and makes it easy to bring the plants indoors for winter use.

Herbs do best in a sunny room, but they like cool temperatures and should not be placed on the windowsill. Indoors, fertilize only once a month with a liquid, natural fertilizer; this light dose of nutrients will keep the plant healthy without promoting new growth so that the highly valued plant oils will remain concentrated in the leaves and stems. (The more oils within the plant, the better it

Use stem cuttings to start **sage** *in the starter tray. Expect the cuttings to root within 3–5 weeks and then to begin producing gray-green, slightly hairy leaves for harvesting.*

Sage.

tastes and smells.) Outdoors, mix dry fertilizer into soil before transplanting. Let pots go almost dry between waterings.

To harvest, snip off the leaves and shoots early in the day, when the flavor is at its best. If you want to dry them for later use, lay the leaves in a warm, airy location (but never in the sun), then put them in a jar and store in a dark place.

Thyme.

Graceful and tall **thyme** *takes about 2–3 weeks to germinate in soil-less mix; stem cuttings can be rooted in peat pellets.*

Herbs are used not only for flavoring, but also in beverages, medicines, dyes, perfumes and insect repellents.

DESCRIPTION: The low, bushy peanut plant does most of its work underground. Its yellow, pea-shaped flowers bend down into the soil, where they develop into the nutlike seeds that we know as peanuts, or "goobers."

For your own peanut harvest, start with "seed" peanuts from a garden center. Do not try planting ordinary peanuts from the grocery store, since these have been specially treated and will not grow. Most gardeners grow Spanish peanuts; if you live in the South, however, you can

Peanut plant.

Peanuts are not nuts at all! Instead, like peas and beans, they're classified as legumes. Their roots are covered with tiny bumps full of bacteria that "fix" nitrogen taken from the air into nitrates, an important nutrient in plant life.

also try Virginia peanuts, which require a longer growing season.

HOW TO PLANT: About 3 weeks before the last frost, remove the shells from the "seed" peanuts, taking care not to tear the "paper" wrappers underneath each shell. Plant only in peat pellets, 2 seeds per pellet. Germination time: 10 days.

GROWING TIPS: Peanut plants grow best in an outdoor garden that has loose, light soil. Transplant outside after all danger of frost is gone and the ground is warm. Spanish seedlings should be spaced 6″ apart; Virginia seedlings, 12″ apart. During the next few weeks, watch closely for the yellow flowers to appear. When they do, carefully loosen the soil around the plants with a hoe in order to make it easier for the flowers to poke their way underground.

When the first frost turns the leaves brown, dig up the peanuts gently with a fork. You'll find dozens of peanut shells hanging on the roots. Brush off the soil, dry the peanuts in the sun, and store them in net bags in a cool place until you're ready to eat them.

Raw peanuts taste terrible, so ask an adult to help you roast them on a lightly greased cookie sheet in a low oven for about 5 minutes.

"Goobers" were first cultivated by Indians in South America.

Outdoor Friends and Foes

Many people look upon all insects as pests, but very few kinds actually attack garden plants. The problem is that this small percentage can multiply if not dealt with immediately. For instance, a single aphid, if left alone, could give rise to two trillion offspring by the end of one growing season!

The best solution is to make your outdoor garden a friendly place for the pests' natural predators. Add a bird bath and keep it filled to attract birds. If at all possible, don't spray with pesticides; as a last resort, use insecticidal soap, which is not poisonous to you or your pets. Finally, leave alone any spiders, toads, frogs, lizards or nonpoisonous snakes that you see in your garden. They eat a lot of pests!

WATCH FOR DISEASE

Most garden sprays that combat disease are extremely poisonous and may result in more harm than good. If your seedlings or plants show any signs of disease—wilting, rotting, mildew, blights or blotches—it's best to cut out the diseased part (or sometimes the whole plant) and throw it away in the garbage. Disinfect the scissors immediately by dipping them in bleach or rubbing alcohol.

Weeds are simply plants that insist on growing where they're not wanted. Often as harmful as garden pests, they compete with your own plants for nutrients, space and water. Hoe your garden once a week, early in the day, to topple young weeds.

Ladybugs and praying mantises, along with hoverflies and many minute wasps, are considered friends because they prey on other insects.

Praying mantis.

Ladybug.

Bug Chart

Be sure to check your plants daily for signs of damage by pests. Some of the most common garden foes are illustrated and described below.

Aphids suck sap, leaving telltale curled-over leaves. **Cure:** *Encourage ladybugs, tiny wasps and the hoverfly by avoiding sprays, or put out plastic strips called "Sticky Stiks."*

The sap-sucking whitefly prefers tomatoes and impatiens. **Cure:** *Encourage tiny wasps by not spraying; try "Sticky Stiks."*

Earwigs, active at night, eat petals and seedlings. **Cure:** *Place 4" squares of corrugated cardboard under leaves; earwigs will hide in the narrow tunnels. Enclose both in plastic bag and dispose of them.*

Slugs and snails eat holes in leaves and roots, leaving behind a glistening slime trail. **Cure:** *These pests will hide under half an eaten grapefruit placed near affected plants in the evening; the next morning, you can enclose bugs and grapefruit in plastic bags and dispose of them.*

Scale looks like tiny brown flattened cones on twigs and stems. **Cure:** *Try insecticidal soap.*

Caterpillars eat leaves and stems. **Cure:** *Remove from plant.*

The tiny spider mite sucks sap, causing powdery, mottled leaves. **Cure:** *Try insecticidal soap.*

Discover the joy and wonder of cultivating flowers! Fill pots and windowboxes, baskets and barrels and garden plots with plants from your Greenhouse. Enjoy their glorious color and scent outdoors, or bring some flowers inside to brighten your home.

Flowers may be *annuals* or *perennials*. Annuals, such as marigolds, grow, flower, get pollinated, go to seed and then die all within one growing season. Perennials, such as tulip bulbs, grow, die back to the ground in the fall, spend the winter underground, and then send up new growth the following spring. "Tender" perennials, such as geraniums, originate in the tropics and cannot stand the frost of northern climates; with care and patience, however, you can help them live through the winter by bringing them indoors.

Geranium.

DESCRIPTION: Bright clusters of geranium flowers—red, salmon, pink or white—are popular additions to any garden. Geraniums are succulents (see page 60), which means they'll flourish under dry conditions that match their native environment of South and East Africa. Ideal for cuttings, the plants also make wonderful cut flowers for indoors and, like most tender perennials, can be "overwintered" as houseplants (see page 43). All geraniums have scented leaves, and some gardeners grow special geraniums only for their smell. Also, the bicolored geraniums, with white throats and red outer petals, are really quite stunning. Look, too, for the ivy-leaf geranium: it's great for hanging baskets and windowboxes.

HOW TO PLANT: Ask a neighbor for a stem cutting from a geranium plant that you like. Cut off any flower buds or extra leaves, then bury the cutting ½″ below the lowest growth on the stem in soil-less mix. Expect it to root within 3–6 weeks.

GROWING TIPS: Transplant into 8″ pots or space 12″ apart in the outdoor garden after all danger of frost is gone. To keep geraniums flowering all season long, gently pinch off the stems of dead blooms where they meet the main stem.

Grow a
Geranium Tree

Set aside one of your cuttings to grow a tall, elegant mini-tree. This project is best done indoors, where the wind can't interfere. Start the cutting in a peat pellet. When it has taken root and the stem has begun to grow, carefully pinch off any side shoots. Leave only the topmost tip of the stem, growing up and up.

When the plant tips over the peat pellet by itself and is "rootbound," growing as tightly as it can within the pellet, transplant it to a 3″ pot and then watch for it to tip itself over again. Each time this happens, transplant the geranium into a bigger pot—until finally it's sitting in a 10″ pot.

When the geranium is 3′ tall, pinch off the growing tip. This will force the plant to break into a bush—or, in this case, a "tree." Now let the next 4 branches develop. When these branches each have 4 leaves, pinch off their growing tips, too. Soon after this, your geranium tree should flower.

When the geranium is 6″ high, start staking the plant. A small bamboo pole is perfect at first. Loosely tie the stalk, just below where a leaf meets the stem, to the stake with a figure-8 knot (see page 23). As the plant reaches its final height of 3′, replace the bamboo stake with a taller, sturdier one.

Some gardeners have grown geranium plants as high as six feet! When the "tree" tips over its pot by itself, it's ready to be repotted.

Impatiens.

Like its wildflower relative the jewelweed, impatiens has seed pods that suddenly burst open if touched, throwing seeds over a wide area. Modern impatiens, however, has been bred to flower—not to produce seeds.

DESCRIPTION: The shade-loving impatiens is "floriferous," which means a single plant produces many, many flowers. Ranging from orange, red and purple to pink and white, the open-faced flowers appear on top of soft, fleshy stems and leaves. Some of these tender annuals ('Rosette,' for example) have double flowers, with petals arranged in many layers.

For low, sprawling plants, look for the 'Elfin' cultivars; for medium-high plants, the 'Blitz' cultivars. The tall New Guinea species has striped or colored leaves as well as lovely flowers, and should grow in a partially sunny location to make the most of them.

HOW TO PLANT: Because the plants take so long to grow, impatiens is best started from stem cuttings. Plant the cuttings in January to be ready for spring transplanting. Expect them to root within 3–5 weeks.

GROWING TIPS: Transplant outside into 6″ or 8″ pots, into hanging baskets or into the garden after all danger of frost is gone. During the growing season, look out for whiteflies and spider mites; if you spot them, check the chart on page 37 for the proper remedies.

Double impatiens blossoms have petals arranged in many layers.

42

Fibrous begonia.

DESCRIPTION: Fibrous begonias are so called because they have fine fibrous roots, unlike the tuberous roots of other garden begonias. These tender perennials are one of the few flowers that can bloom in both sunny and shady conditions, and are rarely damaged by weather or pests. Yellow centers are surrounded by spreading pink, red or white petals, and the whole flower sits on top of three "wings" just below the sepals (the green cup that holds the flower head on top of the stem).

The fleshy leaves come in an assortment of colors. For bronze-tinted leaves, buy 'Rio' cultivars; for green-and-white striped leaves, look for 'Color Queen.' Try 'Pink Avalanche' or 'Viva' (a white begonia) to put in hanging baskets. For begonias that grow just over a foot high, try 'Glamor' cultivars.

HOW TO PLANT: Dustlike begonia seeds are minuscule—an ounce yields over 250,000 plants! For this reason, begonias should be started from cuttings. Expect them to root within 3–5 weeks.

GROWING TIPS: Transplant outside in 6″ pots or space about 8″ apart in a somewhat shady location. Begonias catch mildew disease easily, so try not to splash the leaves as you water the plants.

OVER-WINTERING

Two weeks before the first fall frost, dig up your tender perennials and brush off the soil. Set each in a 6″ pot filled with 2″ of soil-less mix, with the stem base 1″ below the rim. Fill in with mix; press around stem. Cut back to 3–4″ high.

43

Pollination

Flowers are vital to the life of a plant. Buried at the heart of every flower is a nest of tiny ovules that one day, after pollination, will turn into seeds and then, perhaps, one day will grow into full-size plants. To help this process along, most flowers must be visited by insects, birds or other creatures that will unknowingly participate in the pollination process by depositing pollen near the ovules. Thus, flaunting their brilliant colors and sweet scents, flowering plants invite these visitors to drink their nectar, pick up the pollen, and carry it to the ovules.

Here's what happens when a bee, one of the best pollinators on earth, comes to a flower for a drink of nectar.

1. The bee alights on the specialized landing platform of petals, just the right weight for supporting an insect. Special shapes and markings, such as the petunia's trumpet shape or the circular outline of impatiens, guide the bee to the very heart of the flower.

2. The bee takes a drink of nectar and comes in contact with the plant's male reproductive parts: the stamens and pollen. The powdery, yellow pollen waiting on top of the stamens sticks to the bee's legs and furry body.

Most light-colored flowers are pollinated by moths, bats and other nighttime creatures. That's because the pale shades show up better in the dark!

3. When the bee buzzes on to the next flower, the pollen on its body brushes off and is transferred to the female pistil—and pollination takes place. The male pollen travels down inside the pistil to the ovary, where it joins the tiny ovules. Now the flower can begin to make its seeds.

4. After the seedmaking process begins and the flower's job is finished, the petals fall off, the seeds get bigger and bigger, and the ovary swells—sometimes into edible "fruit" such as tomatoes or pumpkins, but often just into small seed pods.

5. Once the seeds are ripe, the plant's next task is to spread them as far and wide as possible. The dandelion, for instance, employs the wind to carry away its seeds on their tiny parachutes. Some plants, such as the burdock, have developed seeds with long barbs on the end, perfect for sticking to animals and people who happen to pass by. Still others, such as sunflowers and corn, rely on animals to eat their seeds and ultimately deposit them in a distant place.

Plants without flashy flowers to act as billboards depend on other methods of pollination. Many rely on the wind to blow the pollen from the male parts of the plant onto the female parts.

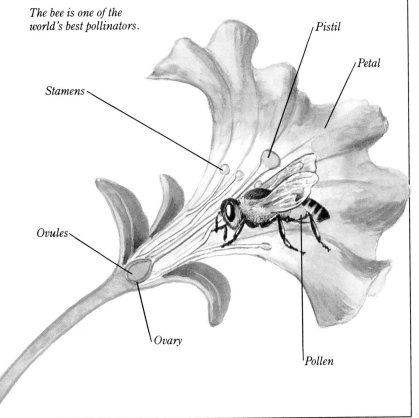

The bee is one of the world's best pollinators.

Pistil

Petal

Stamens

Ovules

Ovary

Pollen

Snapdragon.

DESCRIPTION: The spiky, sturdy snapdragon got its name from the "dragon's face" on each blossom. Pinch one and watch the two velvety lips open wide! Related to the wildflowers called butter-and-eggs or toadflax, these tender perennials range in size from 6″ to 4′ and come in many shades of pink, red and orange, as well as white. Some flowers are bicolored, with two shades on each bloom. Because they can withstand very cool temperatures, snapdragons continue to color your garden into the fall; they also make excellent cut flowers.

Look for 'Rocket Mixed,' 'Madame Butterfly Mixed' or, for dwarf snapdragons, 'Little Darling Mixed.'

HOW TO PLANT: Six weeks before the last frost, spread seeds evenly over soilless mix. Press down firmly; water well. Germination time: 7–10 days.

GROWING TIPS: Transplant into 6″ or 8″ pots, or space 12″ apart in the garden when all danger of frost is gone. Watch the blossoms carefully; whenever all the flowers die on a spike, cut back the spike to keep the plant blooming throughout the growing season.

Look for the dragon's face!

Marigold.

DESCRIPTION: The stocky, hardy marigold, an annual that comes in bright, cheerful shades of yellow, orange and red, makes an excellent cut flower. When you sniff a marigold, you'll notice the strong smell that serves to ward off many insects, especially the soil pests called nematodes; because of this built-in defense mechanism, some people plant marigolds in their garden specifically as a means of pest control.

For dwarf marigolds, about 8″ high, look for 'Bonanza' cultivars. The 'Brocade' and 'Naughty Marietta' cultivars grow about a foot high, while 'Jubilee' cultivars reach a height of 2′. Finally, 'Man in the Moon,' a pale yellow marigold, and any of the 'Climax' cultivars will produce plants 3′ tall.

HOW TO PLANT: Sow the long, spindle-shaped seeds about 8 weeks before planting outside. Use peat pellets, or plant seeds in soil-less mix 2½″ apart and ¼″ deep. Germination time: 5–7 days.

GROWING TIPS: In late spring, transplant seedlings outside 6″ to 12″ apart, depending on the cultivar. Marigolds are "self-breaking," which means the young plant "breaks" off its own growing tip to produce several stems without being pinched back by a gardener.

Bulbs, Bulbs, Bulbs

Some flowers, like tulips and daffodils, grow from swollen underground stems called bulbs. These built-in suitcases of food see the plants through cold or dry spells until they can blossom again the following season. Bulbs have been prized for centuries. In fact, in 1636, a single tulip bulb was worth 80 fat pigs!

Onions and garlic are also bulbs. Ask an adult to cut an onion in half from top to bottom so you can see the scale-like leaf bases surrounding the bulb's inner bud. For a different perspective, look at an onion that has been cut horizontally across the bulb.

An onion is a "true" bulb.

Related to these "true" bulbs are plants like the crocus (actually a corm) and iris (a rhizome). Gardeners call them all bulbs, however, because they store their food in underground stems.

Some types of bulbs are called "tubers." Believe it or not, potatoes are actually the tubers of potato plants. If you leave these underground stems out in daylight, they'll produce chlorophyll and turn green!

Bulbs must have cool temperatures (but above freezing) to flower successfully.

The Green Thumb

"Forcing" Bulbs

For some springtime joy in the middle of winter, buy hyacinth, crocus or paperwhite bulbs that have been specially prepared for indoor planting. These prepared bulbs, which have already had their resting period in simulated winter conditions, will think it's spring when you bring them into the warmth and light of your home!

Generally, you can plant about 6 hyacinth, 8 paperwhite or 12 crocus bulbs in your starter tray. Fill the tray with an even layer of small pebbles or aquarium gravel about 1″ in depth. Nestle the bulbs, pointed end up and flattened base down, into the center of the tray so that they almost touch each other. The top third of the bulbs should be showing. Do not cover with the Greenhouse roof. Bulbs require a cool temperature of about 55°F., so don't place the tray over a radiator; keep it in a north window (away from the sun), and water well.

When planting, make sure the top third of each bulb is showing.

For a spectacular indoor flower during the winter, grow an amaryllis bulb in a 6″ to 8″ clay pot. Fill the pot with soilless mix and plant the bulb "tight," leaving only 1″ between the bulb and the rim of the pot. The top third of the bulb should be visible above the soil. Then follow the care instructions given above for spring bulbs.

White alyssum can be grown in sun or shade, but purple alyssum is only for sunny spots.

DESCRIPTION: The hardy, drought-resistant alyssum hugs the ground as it spreads out in a carpet of tiny, lacy flowers. Renowned for its sweet scent, this annual is excellent for edging flower beds or trailing over the edge of a windowbox.

Buy 'Snow Crystals' for a white cultivar that grows well in both sun and shade. 'Royal Carpet,' a purple cultivar, is only for sunnier locations.

HOW TO PLANT: Sow alyssum seeds about 10 weeks before spring planting. Add bird sand to the seed packet, then sprinkle the mixture over soil-less mix. Press down firmly with your fingers; water gently. Germination time: 7–10 days.

GROWING TIPS: Transplant seedlings 6″ apart into windowboxes or 12″ apart in outdoor gardens. When you clean up your garden beds in the fall, carefully pull up the dead alyssum plants and shake them so the tiny seeds fall onto the soil; if the ground is left undisturbed, seeds may germinate the following spring. Only white alyssum will come up, however, even if you grew purple alyssum the first time around.

Petunia.

DESCRIPTION: Petunias are easy to grow and very versatile. You can plant these annuals in any sunny location, whether in containers or a garden patch, and expect the trumpet-shaped flowers to burst forth regularly. Note the sticky leaves, which discourage insects from attacking the plants.

For bright yellow flowers, look for 'Summer Sun'; for red, 'Comanche' or 'Red Devil'; for purple, 'Sugar Plum' or 'Sugar Daddy'; for pink, 'Apple Blossom' or 'Pink Cloud'; for white, 'Snow Cloud.' Some petunias are double-blossomed, others are striped, and the trailing 'Cascade' cultivars are particularly good for windowboxes or hanging baskets.

HOW TO PLANT: About 10 weeks before the last frost, mix the seeds in the packet with about ½ teaspoon of bird sand and sprinkle over soil-less mix. Press down lightly and water gently, being careful not to wash the seeds away. Germination time: 7–10 days.

GROWING TIPS: Thin seedlings (see page 17) before transplanting into containers. Space about 6″ apart in containers or 1′ apart in an outdoor bed well after the danger of frost is gone. If the petunias get straggly and "leggy," losing their lower leaves, clip their stems halfway back with scissors. New leaves and flowers will sprout within 3 weeks.

Both the petunia and its relative the potato plant originated in the Andes mountains of South America. The petunia produced only small flowers, like potato flowers, until it was bred for the big, showy blooms we enjoy today.

You can eat both the blooms and leaves of the nasturtium plant!

DESCRIPTION: The red, yellow or orange flowers of the nasturtium plant grow against a somewhat straggly background of round, pale green leaves. Both the ruffled flowers and leaves of this annual are edible; they have a slightly peppery taste that makes a delightful addition to salads. Some gardeners use nasturtiums as a "trap crop" on the outside of a garden bed to attract aphids and whitefly (see page 37) in order to keep them away from more valuable crops such as tomatoes.

Look for the hardy, early-blooming 'Whirlibird' cultivar.

HOW TO PLANT: Because it's best not to disturb nasturtium roots when transplanting, sow the big, wrinkled seeds with their light brown papery covering into peat pellets, 2 seeds per pellet. Germination time: 5 days.

GROWING TIPS: Nasturtiums are unusual because they do best in poor soil and don't like to be fertilized. In an "unprepared" part of your garden, plant dwarf cultivars 6″ apart and other cultivars 12″ apart. Water lightly throughout the growing season. Remember that too much food and water will give you lots of foliage but few flowers.

Window Dressings

Potted cascade petunias, alyssum, begonias, geraniums, impatiens and nasturtiums are perfect for transplanting into windowboxes or outdoor hanging baskets. Asparagus fern makes an excellent green foliage plant for both sunny and shady locations.

First decide how much light your windowbox or basket will receive, then choose your flowers accordingly. Half-fill the container with soil-less mix and space plants about 6″ apart. Place taller plants near the center, letting the "trailers" cascade over the edges. Fill in around each plant with mix. When all are in place and the box or basket is full, water thoroughly and add liquid fertilizer.

Windowboxes and baskets tend to dry out very quickly, so your plants will probably require daily watering. (In hot, windy weather, containers should be checked twice a day.) They'll also need fertilizing once a week.

In hot, windy weather, be sure to check outdoor boxes and baskets twice a day.

Grow Some House

Summer or winter, houseplants can add a fresh, living dimension to your home, livening up a corner, windowsill or table while providing an excellent chance to observe plantlife close up. They also act as air fresheners! NASA has shown that a typical spider plant, for example, "cleans" the air of an average-size room by absorbing many gases.

Pay special attention to the amount of water needed by your indoor plants. Watering too heavily or too often can be fatal. (When in doubt, don't!) Most houseplants require a steady diet of liquid fertilizer from early spring to the end of fall.

Dracaena marginata.

DESCRIPTION: The treelike dracaena, one of the hardiest indoor plants you can grow, originated in Africa and Madagascar. Its sword-shaped leaves, which usually emerge from a single stem, can be striped or spotted in assorted colors. Some dracaenas grow quite tall; others, such as 'Gold Dust' and 'Sander's Dracaena,' are more compact and make a good choice for the Greenhouse terrarium (see facing page). 'Gold Dust' is also an exception to the rule, having a bushy shape and oval leaves.

HOW TO PLANT: Plant a cutting in the starter tray, then follow the basic care instructions on page 9; check for rooting in several weeks. For larger cuttings, up to 1' long, place in an 8" pot filled with soilless mix.

GROWING TIPS: Feed with fertilizer once a month. Water only when the mix is almost completely dry to the bottom of the pot. Two cultivars, 'Janet Craig' and 'Warneckii,' may develop brown leaf tips and edges if fluoridated water is used.

Design a Terrarium Garden

To turn your Greenhouse into a terrarium, first line the bottom of your starter tray with a thin sprinkling of crushed charcoal (available at garden centers or made at home by crushing BBQ charcoal yourself). Next add about ½" of soil-less mix. The charcoal will keep the mix from becoming "sour" (which can happen when plants are kept in the same soil without drainage for several months).

Choose 3 small plants for your landscape. For a tall "tree," use a dracaena plant. Add a "bush" with a miniature African violet, 'Watermelon' peperomia or 'Emerald Ripple' peperomia. Last comes the "lawn" or "undergrowth": baby's tears is an excellent ground-hugging plant, as are miniature ferns.

Gently remove the plants from their pots and set them close together in the tray. Depending on the desired effect, surround them with small chunks of broken rock, bark chips, aquarium gravel, bird sand or a combination of these. Do not use dead wood from outside, since it may contain a harmful fungus.

When the garden is finished, spray with water until the mix is soaked through. Then put on the roof and place your terrarium in a bright spot but away from direct sunlight. The water droplets that will form on the roof are from condensation of air vapor; eventually, they'll run down the sides and into the soil. If the plants start growing too big, clip them back with a pair of scissors to keep your landscape lush and tidy.

African violet.

DESCRIPTION: The tidy, compact African violet blooms almost continually, producing velvety flowers in shades of blue, pink, white or even magenta. Choose among varieties that have single, double or semi-double blossoms; leaves, too, vary in shape and color. Try one of the miniatures for something a little different.

HOW TO PLANT: Ask a neighbor if you may take a leaf cutting from a plant you like. Stick the stem of the leaf into a peat pellet or soil-less mix, then follow the instructions for cuttings on page 9. Your cutting will take several months to root properly, but it will make up for lost time once new growth begins. Suddenly, from the base of the leaf, a whole new family of tiny plantlets will pop into sight! Believe it or not, the same stem and leaf can be used again and again until no part of the original leaf stem is left.

GROWING TIPS: Transplant "tight" into a 3″ pot and keep in a bright place but out of direct sunlight; if your plant gets too hot (over 80° F.), it won't flower. A bi-weekly shot of liquid fertilizer will encourage flowering and provide nutrients. Keep the plant moist, but don't splash water on the leaves or they may start to rot. Picking off flowers and leaves immediately after they die will also prevent rot and encourage continuous blooming.

DESCRIPTION: Also known as "Freckleface," this houseplant is originally from Madagascar. After germinating in only 3 days, it eventually grows to about 2' high and produces big green leaves covered with pink spots; by comparison, its dark blue or purple flowers are very small. After the plant is well established, move it out of its sunny location for 2 weeks and you'll see the polkadots begin to fade. The dots only appear in bright light and are at their best in full sun.

The versatile polkadot plant is usually found indoors but can also be seen in outdoor hanging baskets, windowboxes and bordering sunny flower beds.

HOW TO PLANT: Mix some bird sand with the tiny polkadot seeds still in the packet and sprinkle lightly over the surface of soil-less mix. Press down firmly; water gently, taking care not to wash away the seeds. Germination time: 2–3 days.

GROWING TIPS: Transplant seedlings into 6" pots and keep in a sunny location. When plants are 6" high, pinch off tops to promote bushiness.

The polkadot plant develops its best color in full sun.

DESCRIPTION: The tufted desert cactus belongs to a large group of plants called succulents, whose most distinctive trait is their ability to store water. Cactus plants have thick stems specially designed for water retention, while the aloe and other succulents have fleshy leaves that serve the same purpose. Many of these plants produce beautiful flowers and will bloom for you if cared for properly.

HOW TO PLANT: Because its tufts can be needle sharp, cactus should be handled with care. It prefers small pots, so wait several years (until the plant tips over its pot) before transplanting to bigger ones.

GROWING TIPS: Water cactus plants once every 2 weeks in the summer, once every 2 months in the winter; fertilize only in the summer. Dust with a dry paintbrush to avoid getting pricked.

Cereus, a cactus.

Carrion flower, a succulent.

Aloe, a succulent.

The prickly tufts of the cactus help to protect the plant from the hot sun and from animals that want to get to the water inside.

While all cactus are succulents, not all succulents are cactus!

60

Create a Cactus Garden

For a taste of desert living, plan a cactus garden in the starter tray. Select several different little cactus plants, and add another succulent or two for variety.

Fold a single piece of newspaper into a long strip several times and loop it around each cactus. Gripping both paper and cactus, gently pull the plant out of its pot. Place one or two tall cactus plants in the center and surround them with a couple of the rounder, tubbier varieties.

Golden Barrel, a cactus.

Fill in and around the cactus with soil-less mix, then press down pieces of rock around and between the plants. Fill in the smaller spaces with pebbles, and finish off by sprinkling any bare spots with a thin layer of bird sand or aquarium gravel. Spray with water to settle the mix, rocks and sand, and also to give the cactus a good start. Place in a sunny location and follow the growing tips on page 60.

Succulents and cactus can be planted together for a dry, desert garden.

An Outdoor Garden for Beginners

Outdoor gardens, whether plots of ground or big containers like tubs and windowboxes, require a certain amount of planning. Start by drawing the outline of your garden on a blank sheet of notebook paper. Mark which direction is north and which parts of the garden will be shaded by trees. A good size for a beginner's garden is 5' x 5', but you can make adjustments to fit your yard.

Next, make a list of the plants you wish to grow, and check the plant pages before filling in the answers to the following questions.

1. *How much space will each plant need in your garden?* Remember that staking and growing crops up poles can save room for other plants. Be sure to leave space for sprawling plants and for yourself to walk through the rows of plants in your garden.

2. *How much sun or shade does each plant need?* There are not too many vegetables that like shade. Six hours of sun per day is usually considered a minimum for most plants.

3. *How long does each plant need to germinate?* Make a chart so that you'll know in which order to sow your seeds in the starter tray. (If you decide to start with cuttings, ask friends and neighbors ahead of time so they'll have time to help you.)

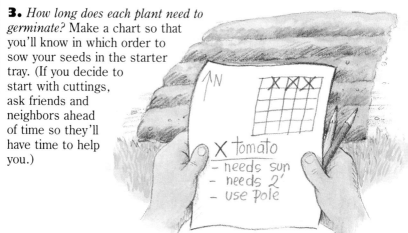

After you decide which plants to grow, draw a color plan of the garden you want.

4. *How long does it take for each plant to grow?* When do you need to plant so your flowers will have enough time to bloom and your vegetables can produce a harvest? In the southern and western United States, where the temperature rarely goes below freezing, you can

From paper to your own real garden.

Mini Vegetable Garden

Mini Vegetable Garden
A. *Cucumbers on stakes*
B. *Tomatoes on stakes*
C. *Lettuce*
D. *Peanuts*
E. *Herbs*

WHEN TO TEST YOUR SOIL

If your plants don't do well even though the light is right and they've been fertilized, watered, and checked for pests and diseases, it's time to test your soil for acidity or akalinity. Ask at your garden center for a "pH kit" such as the Sudbury Garden Soil Tester, and follow the instructions on the package. A pH reading lower than 6.5 requires adding garden lime to your soil to counteract acidity; a reading higher than 7.0 means the soil is alkaline and needs some peat moss, composted pine needles or oak leaves.

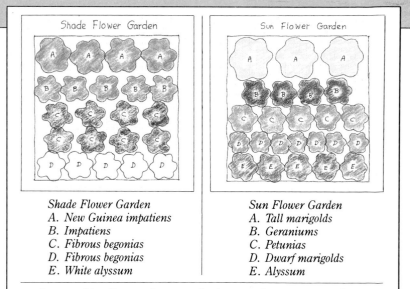

Shade Flower Garden	Sun Flower Garden
Shade Flower Garden A. New Guinea impatiens B. Impatiens C. Fibrous begonias D. Fibrous begonias E. White alyssum	*Sun Flower Garden* A. Tall marigolds B. Geraniums C. Petunias D. Dwarf marigolds E. Alyssum

garden outside all year. In areas farther north, you can garden outdoors only in the spring, summer and fall.

5. Now place an X or a circle inside your garden outline, showing where you plan to place each plant. Put tall plants at the north end so they don't shade the rest of the garden.

Good growing!